scarves
to crochet

edited by Connie Ellison

Annie's
Attic®

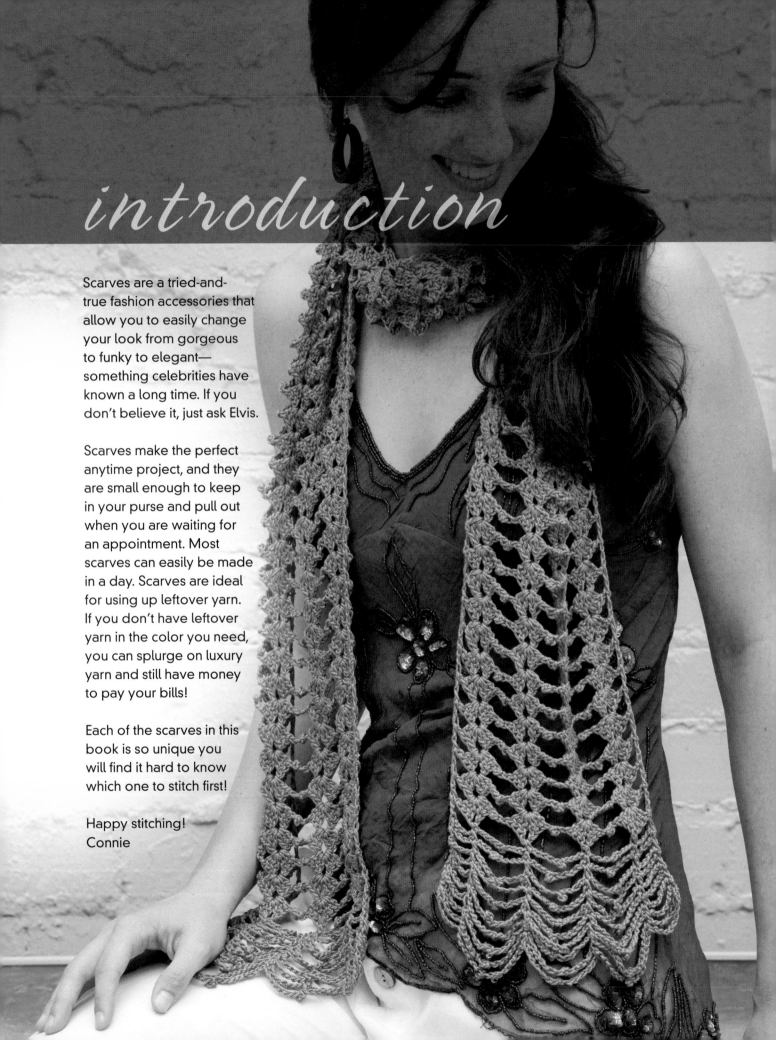

introduction

Scarves are a tried-and-true fashion accessories that allow you to easily change your look from gorgeous to funky to elegant—something celebrities have known a long time. If you don't believe it, just ask Elvis.

Scarves make the perfect anytime project, and they are small enough to keep in your purse and pull out when you are waiting for an appointment. Most scarves can easily be made in a day. Scarves are ideal for using up leftover yarn. If you don't have leftover yarn in the color you need, you can splurge on luxury yarn and still have money to pay your bills!

Each of the scarves in this book is so unique you will find it hard to know which one to stitch first!

Happy stitching!
Connie

contents

4 Floral Fiesta

6 Wasabi Bobbles

8 Hints of Lavender

9 Cape Cod Circles

10 Blocks & Lace

14 Picots in the Sun

16 Gyspy Rose

18 Kiwi Cowl

20 Orange Blossoms

22 Reversible in Blue

24 Grids of Gray

26 Flouncy Shades of Blue

27 Mardi Gras Ribbon

28 Braided Beige

31 Chocolate Truffles

34 Azure Scallops

38 Stitch Guide

39 Metric Conversion Charts

floral fiesta

design by
JENNIFER MCCLAIN

SKILL LEVEL

INTERMEDIATE

FINISHED SIZE

3½ x 80 inches, including Fringe

MATERIALS

- Premier Yarns Deborah Norville Serenity Garden fine (sport) weight yarn (2¼ oz/185 yds/64g per ball): 2 balls #80004 gems
- Schachenmayr Nomotta Catania fine (sport) weight yarn (1¾ oz/137 yds/50g per ball): 1 ball #0209 mandarin
- Size I/9/5.5mm crochet hook or size needed to obtain gauge

GAUGE

9 sts = 2 inches; 2 dc rows = 1 inch

PATTERN NOTE

Leave 7-inch strand when beginning row or fastening off at end of row.

SPECIAL STITCHES

First cable: Ch 3 loosely, sk next 2 sts, sc in next st, **turn,** sc in each of next 3 chs, sl st in next sc (*sc worked directly before ch-3*), **turn,** sc in each of next 2 sk sts.

Cable: Ch 3 loosely, sk next 2 sts (*1 previously worked, 1 previously unworked*), sc in next st, **turn,** sc in each of next 3 chs, sl st in next sc (*sc worked directly before ch-3*), **turn,** sc in each of next 2 sk sts.

Last cable: Ch 3 loosely, sk next 2 sts (*1 previously worked, 1 previously unworked*), sc in next st, **turn,** sc in each of next 3 chs, sl st in next sc (*sc worked directly before ch-3*), **turn,** sc in each of next 2 sk sts, sl st in next sc.

SCARF

Row 1: With gems, ch 303, dc in 4th ch from hook (*3 sk chs count as first dc*), dc in each ch across, turn. (*301 dc*)

Row 2: Ch 3, dc in each st across, turn. Fasten off.

Row 3: Join mandarin with sc in first st, **first cable** (*see Special Stitches*), ***cable** (*see Special Stitches*) across to last 3 sts, **last cable** (*see Special Stitches*), **do not turn.** Fasten off.

Row 4: Join gems with sc in first sc of row 3, ch 3, *working behind cables, dc in each st across, turn.

Row 5: Ch 3, dc in each st across, turn. Fasten off.

Rows 6–8: Rep rows 3–5. At end of last row, **do not fasten off.**

Row 9: Sl st in each st across, fasten off.

Row 10: With RS facing, working on opposite side of chs on row 1, join gems with sl st in first ch, sl st in each ch across. Fasten off.

FRINGE

Cut 60 14-inch strands of gems. With 2 strands held tog, fold strands in half, insert hook in end of row, draw fold through row, draw ends through fold, pull tight. Including 7-inch strands from beg and ends of rows, work 2 Fringes in end of each dc row and 1 Fringe in end of each cable row across each end of Scarf. Trim ends even. ∎

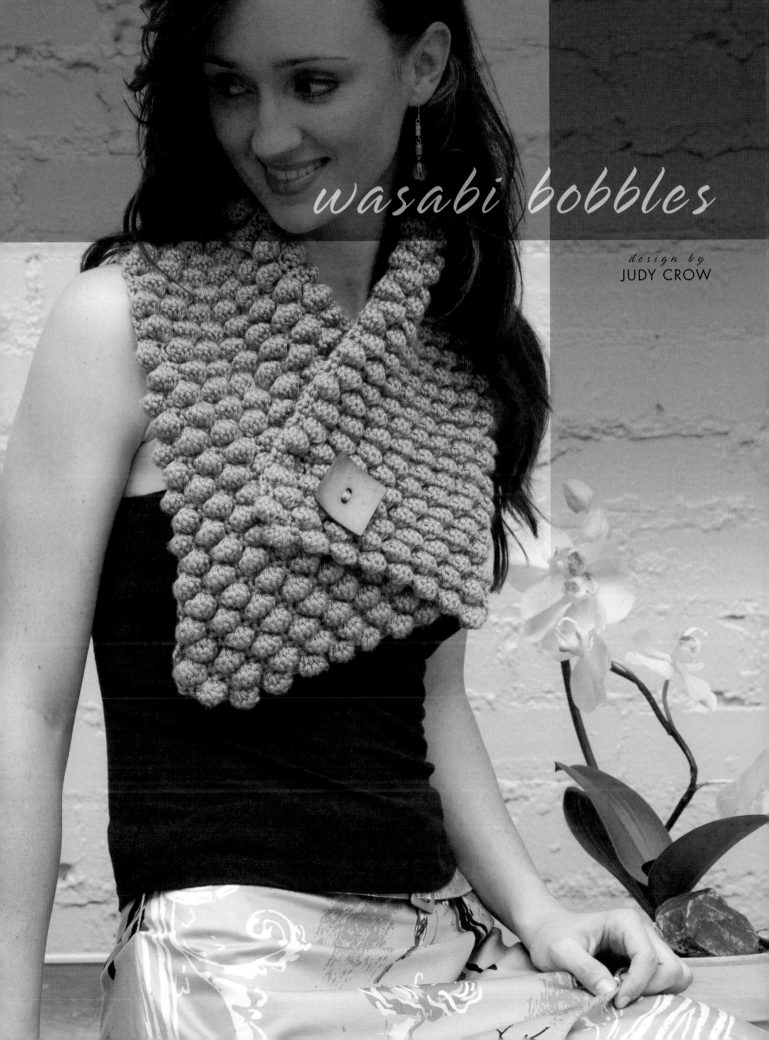

wasabi bobbles

design by
JUDY CROW

SKILL LEVEL

EASY

FINISHED SIZE

7½ x 31½ inches

MATERIALS

- NaturallyCaron.com Country medium (worsted) weight yarn (3 oz/185 yds/85g per ball): 3 balls #0012 foliage
- Size H/8/5mm crochet hook or size needed to obtain gauge
- Dill Creative Buttons 43mm square button: 1 #11006 loden
- 18mm magnetic snaps: 2 antique gold

4
MEDIUM

SPECIAL STITCH

Bobble: Keeping last lp of each st on hook, 5 dc in st indicated, yo, pull through all lps on hook.

SCARF

Row 1: Ch 26, sc in 2nd ch from hook and in each rem ch across, turn.

Row 2: Ch 1, sc in first st, [**bobble** (*see Special Stitch*) in next st, ch 1, sc in each of next 2 sts] across, turn.

Row 3: Ch 1, sc in each sc and in each ch sp across, turn.

Row 4: Ch 1, sc in each of first 2 sts, *bobble in next st, ch 1**, sc in each of next 2 sts, rep from * across, ending last rep at **, sc in last st, turn.

Row 5: Rep row 3.

Rows 6–116: [Rep rows 2–5 consecutively] 28 times, ending last rep with row 4. Fasten off at end of last row.

FINISHING

Sew button to Scarf as shown in photo. Attach 1 half of 1 magnetic snap to right-hand corner of Scarf at end of Scarf with button. Attach rem half of snap to opposite corner at opposite end of Scarf. Attach 1 half of rem snap behind button. Snap first snap tog. Position and attach rem half of 2nd snap to opposite end of Scarf opposite snap half attached behind button. ■

hints of lavender

design by
CAROLYN PFEIFER

SKILL LEVEL

BEGINNER

FINISHED SIZE

Approximately 5 inches wide at center x
48 inches long

MATERIALS

- Plymouth Yarn Jeannee DK light (DK) weight yarn (1¾ oz/136 yds/ 50g per ball):
  2 balls #23 lavender
- Size H/8/5mm crochet hook or size needed to obtain gauge

GAUGE

17 sts = 4 inches; 16 rows = 4 inches

PATTERN NOTES

Work in **back loops** *(see Stitch Guide)* only throughout project.

Chain-2 at beginning of row does not count as a stitch unless otherwise stated.

SCARF

Row 1: Ch 201, hdc in 2nd ch from hook and in each of next 29 chs, sc in each of next 40 chs, hdc in each of next 60 chs, sc in each of next 40 chs, hdc in each of last 30 chs, turn. *(200 sts)*

Row 2: Ch 2, working in **back lps** *(see Pattern Notes)* only, hdc in each of next 30 hdc, sc in each of next 40 sc, hdc in each of next 60 hdc, sc in each of next 40 sc, hdc in each of last 30 hdc, turn.

Next rows: [Rep row 2] 17 times, or until Scarf reaches desired width. At end of last row, fasten off and weave in loose ends. Steam lightly to block. ∎

cape cod circles

design by
RUTHIE MARKS

SKILL LEVEL

EASY

FINISHED SIZE
Approximately 2 x 57 inches

MATERIALS
- Patons Grace light (light worsted) weight yarn (1¾ oz/136 yds/50g per ball):
    1 ball each #62104 azure *(A)*, #62902 spearmint *(B)*, #62027 ginger *(C)*, #62130 sky *(D)* and #62005 snow *(E)*
- Size E/4/3.5mm crochet hook or size needed to obtain gauge

GAUGE
6 dc = 1 inch; 2 dc rnds = 1¼ inches

PATTERN NOTES
For Circles 2–24, pass chain through center of previous Circle before joining at end of round 1.

Repeat color sequence (A-B-C-D-A-B-C-E) 3 times for a total of 24 linked Circles.

Join rounds with slip stitch unless otherwise stated.

Chain-3 at beginning of round counts as first double crochet unless otherwise stated.

SCARF
CIRCLE 1
Rnd 1: Ch 24, being careful not to twist ch, **join** *(see Pattern Notes)* in first ch, **ch 3** *(see Pattern Notes)*, dc in same ch as beg ch-3, 2 dc in each ch around, join in top of beg ch-3. *(48 dc)*

continued on page 37

blocks & lace

design by
RUTHIE MARKS

SKILL LEVEL

■■■■ ▬
EXPERIENCED

FINISHED SIZE
Approximately 4 x 56 inches

MATERIALS
- Patons Silk Bamboo light (light worsted) weight yarn (2¼ oz/ 102 yds/65g per ball):
  1 ball each #85219 sea (*A*), #85510 apricot (*B*), #85107 sapphire (*C*), #85511 coral (*D*), #85010 almond (*E*) and #85008 ivory (*F*)
- Size E/4/3.5mm and K/10½/6.5mm crochet hooks or size needed to obtain gauge
- Stitch markers: 2

GAUGE
Size K hook: 7 sc = 2 inches; 5 rows = 2 inches

PATTERN NOTES
When a color is dropped at the end of a row, place a marker in the elongated loop before moving on to the next row. To begin the next same-color row, remove the marker and insert the hook to continue.

Clusters are only worked on rows where the hook is inserted from the top down. In the first set of cluster rows 44–51, for example, clusters are made on rows 44 and 48 (first and 3rd rows) with E on side 1, and on rows 47 and 51 (2nd and 4th rows) with F on side 2.

SPECIAL STITCHES
Top link single crochet (top link sc): Working from top down, sc in indicated lp of indicated st 1 row below and in indicated lp of indicated st 2 rows below.

Bottom link single crochet (bottom link sc): Working from bottom up, sc in indicated lp of indicated st 2 rows below and in indicated lp of indicated st 1 row below.

Top link cluster (top link cl): Working from top down, keeping last lp of each st on hook, 4 dc in indicated lp of indicated st 1 row below and in indicated lp of indicated st 2 rows below, yo, draw through all lps on hook.

Beginning cluster (beg cl): Ch 3, dc in same place as beg ch-3.

Cluster (cl): Keeping last lp of each st on hook, 3 dc in indicated st, yo, draw through all lps on hook.

2-dc cluster (2-dc cl): Keeping last lp of each st on hook, 2 dc in indicated st, yo, draw through all lps on hook.

SCARF
Row 1: With larger hook and A, ch 16, sc in 2nd ch from hook and in each rem ch across, turn. (*15 sc*)

Row 2: Ch 1, sc in **front lp** (*see Stitch Guide*) of each sc across, drop A, **place marker** (*see Pattern Notes*), **do not turn.**

Row 3: Join B with **top link sc** (*see Special Stitches*) in **back lp** (*see Stitch Guide*) of next st 1 row below and rem lp of next st 2 rows below, *top link sc in back lp of next st 1 row below and in rem lp of next st 2 rows below, rep from * across, drop B, place marker, pick up A, turn.

Row 4: With A, ch 1, *top link sc in back lp of next st 1 row below and in rem lp of next st 2 rows below, rep from * across, drop A, place marker, pick up B, do not turn.

Row 5: With B, ch 1, ***bottom link sc** (*see Special Stitches*) in rem lp of next st 2 rows below and in front lp of next st 1 row below, rep from * across, drop B, place marker, pick up A, turn.

Row 6: With A, ch 1, *bottom link sc in rem lp of next st 2 rows below and in front lp of next st 1 row below, rep from * across, drop A, place marker, pick up B, do not turn.

Row 7: With B, ch 1, *top link sc in back lp of next st 1 row below and in rem lp of next st 2 rows below, rep from * across, drop B, place marker, pick up A.

Rows 8–23: [Rep rows 4–7 consecutively] 4 times. At end of last row, pick up C.

Row 24: With C, ch 1, *top link sc in back lp of next st 1 row below and in rem lp of next st 2 rows below, rep from * across, drop C, place marker, pick up D, do not turn.

Row 25: With D, ch 1, *bottom link sc in rem lp of next st 2 rows below and in front lp of next st 1 row below, rep from * across, drop D, place marker, pick up C, turn.

Row 26: With C, ch 1, *bottom link sc in rem lp of next st 2 rows below and in front lp of next st 1 row below, rep from * across, drop C, place marker, pick up D, do not turn.

Row 27: With D, ch 1, *top link sc in back lp of next st 1 row below and in rem lp of next st 2 rows below, rep from * across, drop D, place marker, pick up C.

Rows 28–43: [Rep rows 24–27 consecutively] 4 times. At end of last row, pick up E.

Row 44: With E, ch 1, top link sc in back lp of next st 1 row below and in rem lp of next st 2 rows below, ***top link cl** (see Special Stitches) in back lp of next st 1 row below and in rem lp of next st 2 rows below**, [top link sc in back lp of next st 1 row below and in rem lp of next st 2 rows below] 3 times, rep from * across, ending last rep at **, top link sc in back lp of next st 1 row below and in rem lp of next st 2 rows below, drop E, place marker, pick up F, do not turn.

Row 45: With F, ch 1, *bottom link sc in back lp of next st 1 row below and in rem lp of next st 2 rows below, rep from * across, drop F, place marker, pick up E, turn.

Row 46: With E, ch 1, *bottom link sc in rem lp of next st 2 rows below and in front lp of next st 1 row below, rep from * across, drop E, place marker, pick up F, do not turn.

Row 47: With F, ch 1, top link sc in rem lp of next st 2 rows below and in front lp of next st 1 row below, *top link cl in rem lp of next st 2 rows below and in front lp of next st 1 row below**, [top link sc in rem lp of next st 2 rows

below and in front lp of next st 1 row below] 3 times, rep from * across, ending last rep at **, top link sc in rem lp of next st 2 rows below and in front lp of next st 1 row below, drop F, place marker, pick up E, turn.

Rows 48–51: Rep rows 44–47. At end of last row, pick up A.

Rows 52–71: Alternating A and B, [rep rows 4–7 consecutively] 5 times. At end of last row, pick up C.

Rows 72–91: Alternating C and D, [rep rows 4–7 consecutively] 5 times. At end of last row, pick up E.

Rows 92–99: Rep rows 44–51.

Rows 100–195: [Rep rows 52–99 consecutively] twice.

Rows 196–235: Rep rows 52–91.

At the end of last row, do not fasten off D, turn.

EDGING
FIRST END
Row 1: With size E hook, ch 1, 2 sc in each st across, turn. *(30 sc)*

Row 2: Ch 1, sc in first sc, *ch 1, sk next sc, sc in next sc, rep from * across, sc in last sc, turn.

Row 3: Ch 1, sc in first sc, ch 5, *sk next sc, ch-1 sp and sc, sc in next ch-1 sp, ch 5, rep from * across to last ch-1 sp, sc in last ch-1 sp and in last sc, turn. *(9 sc, 7 ch-5 sps)*

Row 4: **Beg cl** *(see Special Stitches)* in first sc, *ch 3, sc in next ch-5 sp, ch 2**, **cl** *(see Special Stitches)* in next sc, rep from * 5 times, ending last rep at **, **2-dc cl** *(see Special Stitches)* in last sc, turn.

Row 5: Ch 6, sc in first ch-2 sp, ch 5, sc in next ch-3 sp, [ch 5, sc in next ch-2 sp, ch 5, sc in next ch-3 sp] 6 times, ch 2, dc in top of beg cl, turn. *(14 ch sps)*

Rows 6–8: *Ch 5, sc in next ch-5 sp, rep from * across, turn. *(15 sc, 14 ch-5 sps at end of last row)*

Row 9: Ch 1, sc in first sc, *5 sc in next ch-5 sp, sc in next sc, rep from * 12 times, 5 sc in last ch-5 sp, sl st in beg ch. Fasten off.

2ND END
Row 1: With size E hook, join A with sc in opposite side of foundation ch, ch 1, 2 sc in each st across, turn. *(30 sc)*

Rows 2–9: Rep rows 2–9 of First End. Fasten off.

Weave in ends. ■

picots in the sun

design by
JUDY CROW

SKILL LEVEL
EASY

FINISHED SIZE
5 x 62 inches, excluding tassels

MATERIALS

- Red Heart Bamboo Wool medium (worsted) weight yarn (1¾ oz/87 yds/50g per ball):
  3 balls #3265 gold
- Size H/8/5mm crochet hook or size needed to obtain gauge

GAUGE
3 tr = 1 inch; 4 sc = 1 inch; 4 rows = 2½ inches

PATTERN NOTE
Chain-4 at beginning of row counts as first treble crochet unless otherwise stated.

SPECIAL STITCH
Picot: Ch 3, sl st in last sc made.

SCARF
Row 1: Ch 22, tr in 5th ch from hook, ch 3, sk next 3 chs, [tr in each of next 3 chs, ch 3, sk next 3 chs] across to last 2 chs, tr in each of last 2 chs, turn.

Row 2: Ch 1, sc in each of first 2 tr, *sc in each of next 2 chs, **picot** *(see Special Stitch)*, sc in next ch**, sc in each of next 3 tr, rep from * across, ending last rep at **, sc in next tr, sc in 4th ch of beg 4 sk chs, turn.

Row 3: **Ch 4** *(see Pattern Note)*, tr in next sc, ch 3, sk next 3 sc, [tr in each of next 3 sc, ch 3, sk next 3 sc] across to last 2 sc, tr in each of last 2 sc, turn.

Next rows: [Rep rows 2 and 3 alternately] 103 times or until Scarf reaches desired length.

Last row: Rep row 2. Fasten off; weave in ends.

continued on page 37

gypsy rose

design by
JUDY CROW

SKILL LEVEL

EASY

FINISHED SIZE
Flower: 5 inches in diameter

MATERIALS
- Bulky (chunky) weight yarn:
  50 yds color of choice
- Medium (worsted) weight yarn:
  50 yds each 2 colors of choice
- Light (light worsted) weight yarn:
  50 yds each 2 colors of choice
- Size H/8/5mm crochet hook
- 6mm pony beads:
  28 (or amount desired) beads in
  coordinating color of choice
  36 (or amount desired) beads in
  coordinating color of choice
- 2-inch diameter cloth-covered elastic
  ponytail holder

5 BULKY

4 MEDIUM

3 LIGHT

GAUGE
Gauge is not necessary for this project.

SPECIAL STITCHES
Bead chain (bead ch): Slide bead up close to
previous ch, yo, complete ch.

Bead double crochet (bead dc): Yo, push bead to
top of hook, insert the hook in indicated st,
pull lp through, with bead in center, yo, pull
through 2 lps, yo, pull through 2 lps.

FLOWER
Rnd 1: With worsted weight yarn, join with **sl st
around ponytail holder** (*see illustration*), [ch
12, sl st around ponytail holder] 25 times, **do
not join or turn.**

Rnd 2: Sl st between next 2 sl sts, [ch 18, sl st
between next 2 sl sts] 22 times. Fasten off.

STRANDS
*Note: Using options listed below, make as many
or as few strands as desired.*

CHAIN ONLY
Using yarn of choice, join with sl st around
ponytail holder, ch as many as desired.
Fasten off.

STITCHES ONLY
Using yarn of choice, join with sl st around
ponytail holder, ch as many as desired, 2 sc in
2nd ch from hook and in each rem ch across,
join in beg sl st.

CHAINS & BEADS
Using yarn of choice, thread 28 beads on yarn,
join with sl st around ponytail holder, [ch 6,
bead ch (*see Special Stitches*)] 28 times or until
all beads are used, ch 6, fasten off.

STITCHES & BEADS
Using yarn of choice, thread 36 beads on yarn,
join with sl st around ponytail holder, ch 108
(or number of pony beads multiplied by 3),
ch 6, dc in 4th ch from hook and in each of next
2 chs, [**bead dc** (*see Special Stitches*) in next ch,
dc in each of next 2 chs] across until all beads
are used, dc in each rem ch, join in beg sl st.
Fasten off. ■

A

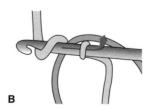
B

C

Slip Stitch Around Ponytail Holder

kiwi cowl

design by
RUTHIE MARKS

SKILL LEVEL

EASY

FINISHED SIZE

Approximately 14½ inches wide x 40 inches in circumference

MATERIALS

- Patons Angora Bamboo medium (worsted) weight yarn (1¾ oz/80 yds/50g per ball):
  7 balls #90243 laurel leaf
- Size H/8/5mm crochet hook or size needed to obtain gauge

GAUGE

3 cls = 2 inches; 6 rows = 2 inches

SPECIAL STITCH

Cluster (cl): (Sc, hdc, sc) in indicated st.

COWL

Row 1: Ch 69, ***cl** *(see Special Stitch)* in 3rd ch from hook, sk next 2 chs, rep from * across to last ch, cl in last ch, turn. *(23 cl)*

Row 2: Ch 1, cl in **back lp** *(see Stitch Guide)* of each hdc across, turn.

Rows 3–9: Rep row 2.

Row 10: Ch 1, (sc, hdc, sc) in both lps of each hdc across, turn.

Rows 11 & 12: Rep row 10.

Rows 13–21: Rep row 2.

Rows 22–24: Rep row 10.

Rows 25–120: [Rep rows 13–24 consecutively] 8 times.

Row 121 (joining row): With rows 120 and 1 held tog, working through both thicknesses, ch 1, sl st in both lps of first hdc and opposite side of foundation ch, *ch 2, sl st in both lps of next hdc and in opposite side of next foundation ch, rep from * across. Fasten off.

Weave in ends. ■

orange blossoms

design by
RUTHIE MARKS

SKILL LEVEL

EASY

FINISHED SIZE

Approximatelyimately 5 x 42 inches

MATERIALS

- Plymouth Yarn Encore Worsted medium (worsted) weight yarn (3½ oz/200 yds/100g per ball): 2 balls #1383 bright orange
- Size H/8/5mm crochet hook or size needed to obtain gauge

GAUGE

11 tr and 10 ch-1 sps = 5 inches; 3 sc rows and 1 tr row = 1½ inches

SPECIAL STITCH

Curlicue: Ch 4, 2 sc in 2nd ch from hook and in each of next 2 chs.

SCARF

Row 1: Ch 22, sc in 2nd ch from hook, *ch 1, sk 1 ch, sc in next ch, rep from * across, turn. *(11 sc)*

Row 2: Ch 1, sc in first sc, *ch 1, sc in next sc, rep from * across, turn. *(11 sc)*

Row 3: Ch 5 *(counts as tr and ch-1)*, sk first 2 sts, tr in next sc, *ch 1, tr in next sc, rep from * across, turn. *(11 tr)*

Row 4: Ch 1, sc in first tr, *ch 1, sc in next tr, rep from * across, sc in 4th ch of beg ch-5, turn. *(11 sc)*

Row 5: Ch 1, sc in first sc, *ch 1, sc in next sc, rep from * across, turn. *(11 sc)*

Rows 6–26: [Rep rows 3–5 consecutively] 7 times.

Rows 27 & 28: Rep rows 3 and 4.

Row 29: Ch 1, sc in each sc and ch-1 sp across, turn. *(21 sc)*

Row 30: Ch 5, sk first 2 sts, tr in next sc, [ch 1, tr in next tr] 3 times, ch 11, sk next 11 sc, tr in next tr, [ch 1, tr in next tr] 3 times, turn. *(8 tr)*

Row 31: Ch 1, sc in each st and ch across, sc in 4th ch of beg ch-5, turn. *(21 sc)*

Row 32: Ch 1, sc in first sc, *ch 1, sk next sc, sc in next sc, rep from * across, turn. *(11 sc)*

Rows 33–83: [Rep rows 3–5 consecutively] 17 times. Fasten off at end of last row.

FLOWERS
SMALL 5-PETAL
MAKE 6.

Rnd 1: Ch 2, 10 sc in 2nd ch from hook, **do not join.**

Rnd 2: (Sc, hdc, dc, hdc, sc) in first sc, *sk next sc, (sc, hdc, dc, hdc, sc) in next sc, rep from * around to last sc, sl st in last sc. Fasten off.

LARGE CURLICUE
MAKE 4.

Rnd 1: Ch 2, 7 sc in 2nd ch from hook, **do not join.**

Rnd 2: Sc in first sc, **curlicue** *(see Special Stitch)*, [sc in next sc, curlicue] 6 times.

Rnd 3: Sc in first sc, [ch 5, working behind next curlicue, sc in next sc] 7 times.

Rnd 4: [Sc, hdc, dc, 3 tr, dc, hdc, sc] in each ch-5 sp around, join with sl st in first sc. Fasten off.

For hair flower make 1 small flower and attach to a ponytail holder. ■

reversible in blue

design by
MARGARET HUBERT

SKILL LEVEL

EXPERIENCED

FINISHED SIZE
8 x 50 inches

MATERIALS
- Lion Brand LB Collection Silk Mohair super fine (fingering) weight yarn (¾ oz/231 yd/25g per ball):
  1 ball #106 azure (CC)
- Lion Brand LB Collection Cashmere light (DK) weight yarn (¾ oz/82 yards/25g per ball):
  4 balls #106 cruise (MC)
- Size H/8/5mm crochet hook or size needed to obtain gauge

GAUGE
4 shells = 5 inches

PATTERN NOTES
Scarf is worked in 2 colors, which are carried up sides.

Scarf is worked in two 25-inch pieces and sewn together at back of neck.

Pattern is worked in a multiple of 8 stitches plus 1.

SPECIAL STITCH
Shell: 5 dc in indicated place.

SCARF
HALF
MAKE 2.
Row 1: With MC, ch 33, dc in 5th ch from hook, **shell** (see Special Stitch) in next ch, dc in next ch, *sk next 2 chs, dc in next ch, 3 dc in next ch, dc in next ch, rep from * across to last ch, leave last ch unworked, draw up long lp, drop lp from hook, **do not turn.** (6 shells)

Row 2: Join CC in 2nd ch of beg 4 sk chs, working in front of last row, *ch 6, sk next shell, sc in first ch of next 2 sk chs on the beg ch, rep from * across to unworked ch of row 1, ch 6, sc in last ch, turn.

Row 3: With CC, ch 2, sl st in first dc of last shell, ch 2, *working through both thicknesses, 5 dc in next ch-6 sp 1 row below and in center st of next shell 2 rows below, rep from * across, sc around beg ch at end of row, draw up long lp, drop lp from hook, **do not turn.**

Row 4: Place dropped MC lp on hook, *ch 6, working in front of last shell-st row (1 row below), sk next CC shell, sc in natural sp between shells of CC row, rep from * across, sc around beg ch at end of row, turn.

Row 5: With MC, ch 2, sl st in first dc of last shell-st row, ch 2, *working through both thicknesses, 5 dc in next ch-6 sp 1 row below and in center st of next shell 2 rows below, rep from * across, draw up long lp, drop lp from hook, **do not turn.**

Row 6: Place dropped CC lp on hook, working in front of last row, *ch 6, sk next MC shell and work sc in natural sp between shells of MC row, rep from * across, sc around beg ch at end of row.

Next rows: [Rep rows 2–5 consecutively] until pattern measures 25 inches from beg, ending with MC shell row. Fasten off at end of last row.

FINISHING
Sew both halves tog, leaving scalloped edges for each short end of Scarf.

Block Scarf by laying flat on a padded surface; spritz lightly with water, pat into shape. Allow to dry. ■

grids of gray

design by
SHANNON MULLET-BOWLSBY

SKILL LEVEL

EASY

FINISHED SIZE

Approximately 6½ x 58 inches

MATERIALS

- Bernat Satin medium (worsted) weight yarn (3½ oz/200 yds/100g per ball):
  1 ball each #04044 stone (*A*) and #04045 grey mist heather (*B*)
- Size G/6/4mm crochet hook or size needed to obtain gauge

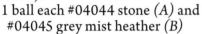

GAUGE

5 dc = 1½ inches; 3 rows = 1½ inches

PATTERN NOTE

Do not turn at ends of rows. Each row is worked with right side facing.

SCARF

Row 1 (RS): With A, ch 21, working in **back bar of chs** (*see illustration*), sc in 2nd ch from hook and in each of next 18 chs, (sc, sl st) in next ch, ch 221, working in back bar of chs, sc in 2nd ch from hook and in each of next 19 chs. Fasten off. **Do not turn** (*see Pattern Note*).

Back Bar of Chain

Row 2 (RS): With B, ch 21, working in back bar of chs, sc in 2nd ch from hook and in each of next 19 chs, dc in back bar of each of last 5 chs before 2nd group of 20 sc on row 1, [ch 10, sk next 10 chs on row 1, dc in back bar of each of next 5 chs on row 1] 13 times, ch 21, working in back bar of chs, sc in 2nd ch from hook and in each of next 19 chs. Fasten off. Do not turn.

Row 3 (RS): With A, ch 21, working in back bar of chs, sc in 2nd ch from hook and in each of next 19 chs, dc in each of first 5 dc in previous row [ch 10, sk next 10 chs on previous row, dc in each of next 5 sts] 13 times, ch 21, working in back bar of chs, sc in 2nd ch from hook and in each of next 19 chs. Fasten off. Do not turn.

Row 4: With A, rep row 3.

Rows 5 & 6: With B, rep row 3.

Row 7: With A, rep row 3.

Row 8: With B, rep row 3.

Row 9: With A, rep row 3.

Rows 10 & 11: With B, rep row 3.

Rows 12 & 13: With A, rep row 3.

Row 14: With B, rep row 3.

FINISHING

Block. Weave in all ends. ■

flouncy shades of blue

design by
DOROTHY WARRELL

SKILL LEVEL

EASY

FINISHED SIZE
5 x 54 inches

MATERIALS
- Patons Lace fine (sport) weight yarn (3 oz/498 yds/85g per ball): 1 ball #33129 porcelain
- Size I/9/5.5mm crochet hook or size needed to obtain gauge

GAUGE
6 sc = 2 inches; rnds 1 and 2 = 1 inch in diameter

PATTERN NOTE
Join rounds with slip stitch unless otherwise stated.

SCARF

Rnd 1: Ch 151, sc in 2nd ch from hook and in each rem ch across to last ch, 3 sc in last ch, working in opposite side of chs, sc in each of next 40 chs, ch 10, sk next 10 chs, sc in each rem ch across to last ch, 2 sc in last ch, **join** (*see Pattern Note*) in first sc, turn.

Rnd 2: Ch 1, sc in each sc around to ch-10, sc in each of next 10 chs, sc in each sc across to 2nd sc of next 3-sc group, 3 sc in next sc, sc in each rem sc around, **do not turn**.

Rnd 3: Sc in each st around to 2nd sc of next 3-sc group, (sc, ch 4, 2 tr) in next sc, tr in each sc around to 2nd sc of next 3-sc group, 3 tr in next sc, tr in each rem st around, join in top of ch-4.

continued on page 37

mardi gras ribbon

design by
RUTHIE MARKS

SKILL LEVEL

EASY

FINISHED SIZE

Approximately 58 inches long, before knotting

MATERIALS

- Lion Brand Incredible super bulky (super chunky) weight yarn (1¾ oz/ 110 yds/50g per ball): 2 balls #205 carnival

SUPER BULKY

- Sizes K/10½/6.5mm and L/11/8mm crochet hooks or size needed to obtain gauge

GAUGE

Size K hook: 14 sl sts = 4 inches

PATTERN NOTE

When crocheting into **chains**, work loosely and in top loops only.

STRANDS
MAKE 5.

With size K hook, ch 200, 4 sc in 2nd ch from hook, 4 sc in each of next 11 chs, sl st in same ch as last 4 sc, sl st in each rem ch across, ch 13, 4 sc in 2nd ch from hook, 4 sc in each of next 11 chs, sl st in same ch as last 4 sc, sl st in last sl st worked in ch. Fasten off.

TUBE

Row 1: With size L hook, ch 21, sc in 2nd ch from hook and in each rem ch across, turn. *(20 sc)*

Rows 2–7: Ch 1, sc in each sc across, turn. **Do not fasten off** at end of last row.

continued on page 37

braided beige

design by
DARLA SIMS

SKILL LEVEL

EASY

FINISHED SIZE

Approximately 6½ inches wide x 25 inches in diameter, after assembly

MATERIALS

- Bernat Satin medium (worsted) weight yarn (3½ oz/200 yds/ 100g per ball):
  3 balls #04010 camel
- Size H/8/5mm crochet hook or size needed to obtain gauge
- Safety pin

4 MEDIUM

GAUGE

8 sts = 4 inches; 12 rows = 4 inches

PATTERN NOTES

Scarf is worked as three separate Strips which are braided together.

Chain-2 counts as first half double crochet unless otherwise stated.

SPECIAL STITCHES

Knot: [Yo, insert hook around post of indicated st and pull up lp] 3 times, yo, pull through all 7 lps on hook

Front post double crochet decrease (fpdc dec): Keeping last lp of each st on hook, fpdc around indicated sts, yo, draw through all lps on hook.

Knot decrease (knot dec): Keeping all lps on hook, knot around indicated sts, yo, draw through all lps on hook.

SCARF
KNOTTED OVAL STRIP
MAKE 1.

Row 1 (RS): Ch 12, working in **back bar of each ch** (*see illustration*), hdc in 3rd ch from hook and in each rem ch across, turn. (*11 hdc*)

Back Bar of Chain

Row 2 (WS): Ch 1, hdc in each st across, turn.

Row 3: Ch 1, hdc in first st, **fpdc** (*see Stitch Guide*) around next hdc 1 row below, hdc in each of next 3 sts on current row, **knot** (*see Special Stitches*) around post of next hdc 1 row below next st, hdc in each of next 3 sts on current row, fpdc around hdc below next st, hdc in last st, turn.

Row 4: Ch 1, hdc in each st across, turn.

Row 5: Ch 1, hdc in first st, fpdc around next fpdc, hdc in next st, 2 fpdc around top of next knot, hdc in next st, 2 fpdc around same knot, hdc in next st, fpdc around next fpdc, hdc in last st, turn.

Row 6: Rep row 4.

Row 7: Ch 1, hdc in first st, fpdc around next fpdc, hdc in next st, fpdc around each of next 2 fpdc, hdc in next st, fpdc around each of next 2 fpdc, hdc in next st, fpdc around each of next 2 fpdc, hdc in next st, fpdc around next fpdc, hdc in last st, turn.

Rows 8 & 9: Rep rows 4 and 7.

Row 10: Rep row 4.

Row 11: Ch 1, hdc in first st, fpdc around next fpdc, hdc in each of next 3 sts, **fpdc dec** (*see Special Stitches*) around next 4 fpdc, hdc in each of next 3 sts, fpdc around next fpdc, hdc in last st, turn.

Row 12: Rep row 4.

Row 13: Ch 1, hdc in first st, fpdc around next fpdc, hdc in each of next 3 sts, **knot dec** (*see Special Stitches*) around next 4 fpdc, hdc in each of next 3 sts, fpdc around next fpdc, hdc in last st, turn.

Rows 14–151: [Rep rows 4–13 consecutively] 14 times, ending last rep with row 11.

Fasten off at end of last row. Strip should measure approx 50 inches long.

DIP-ST STRIP
MAKE 2.

Row 1 (RS): Ch 12, working in back bar of each ch, sc in 2nd ch from hook, *ch 1, sk next ch, sc in next ch, rep from * across, turn.

Row 2 (WS): Ch 2 *(see Pattern Notes)*, dc in next sk ch 1 row below, *ch 1, sk next sc, dc in next sk ch 1 row below, rep from * ending with hdc in last st, turn.

Row 3: Ch 2, dc in next sk sc 1 row below, *ch 1, sk next dc, dc in next sk sc 1 row below, rep from * across to last 2 sts, ch 1, sk next dc, hdc in last st, turn.

Row 4: Ch 2, dc in next sk dc 1 row below, *ch 1, sk next dc, dc in next sk dc 1 row below, rep from * across to last 2 sts, ch 1, sk next dc, hdc in last st, turn.

Next rows: Rep row 4 until Dip-St Strip measures same length as Knotted Oval Strip.

Last row: Ch 1, sc in each hdc or dc, dc in next sk dc 1 row below. Fasten off.

Weave in ends

ASSEMBLY

Using safety pin to hold 1 end of each Strip tog, braid Strips tog. Holding both ends of each Strip tog, working through both thicknesses, sew ends of each Strip tog. Fasten off. Weave in ends. ∎

chocolate truffles

design by
JENNIFER MCCLAIN

SKILL LEVEL

INTERMEDIATE

FINISHED SIZE

3½ x 70 inches, including Tassels

MATERIALS

- Lion Brand Vanna's Glamour fine (sport) weight yarn (1¾ oz/ 202 yds/50g per ball):
  1 ball #134 copper
- Lion Brand Fun Fur bulky (chunky) weight yarn (1¾ oz/64 yds/ 50g per ball):
  1 ball #126 chocolate
- Size I/9/5.5mm crochet hook or size needed to obtain gauge
- 6 x 11-inch cardboard piece

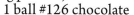

2 FINE

5 BULKY

GAUGE

2 star sts = 1 inch; 1 star st row = 1 inch

PATTERN NOTES

Leave 12-inch length when beginning rows with new color or fastening off previous color.

Join with slip stitch unless otherwise stated.

SPECIAL STITCHES

First beginning star stitch (first beg star st):
  Keeping all lps on hook, yo, insert hook in 3rd ch from hook, yo, draw lp through, sk next ch, yo, insert hook in next ch, yo, draw lp through (*5 lps on hook*), yo, draw through all lps on hook.

First Beginning Star Stitch

Beginning star stitch (beg star st): Yo, insert hook in next st, yo, draw lp through, sk next st, yo, insert hook in next st, yo, draw lp through (*5 lps on hook*), yo, draw through all lps on hook.

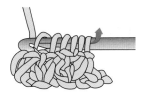

Beginning Star Stitch

Star stitch (star st): Keeping all lps on hook, yo, insert hook in same ch or st as last st of previous star st, yo, draw lp through, sk next ch or st, insert hook in next ch or st, draw lp through, yo, draw through all 5 lps on hook.

Star Stitch

SCARF

Row 1: With copper, **leaving 12-inch length** (*see Pattern Notes*), ch 251, **first beg star st** (*see Special Stitches*), *ch 1, **star st** (*see Special Stitches*), rep from * across, turn. (*124 star sts*)

Row 2: Ch 3, **beg star st** (*see Special Stitches*), *ch 1, star st, rep from * across. **Leaving 12-inch end** (*see Pattern Notes*), fasten off.

Row 3: **Join** (*see Pattern Notes*) chocolate in first st of last row, sl st in each st across. Fasten off.

Row 4: Join copper in **back lp** (*see Stitch Guide*) of first st on last row, sl st in each st across, turn.

Row 5: Ch 1, sl st in first st, sc in next st, hdc in next st, ch 1, star st across to last 3 sts, hdc in next st, sc in next st, sl st in last st, turn.

Row 6: Sk first st, sl st in first sc, hdc in next hdc, now working in ch-1 sps, star st across to last 3 sts, hdc in next st, sl st in next st,. Leaving rem st unworked. Fasten off.

Row 7: Working on opposite side of ch on row 1, rep row 3.

Rows 8–10: Rep rows 4–6.

Rnd 11: Now working in rnds around entire outer edge of Scarf, join chocolate in first st of row 10, sl st in each st and evenly sp across ends of rows around, join in first st. Fasten off.

TASSEL
MAKE 2.
Wrap copper around 11-inch length of cardboard 20 times, forming 40 strands, each 11 inches long. Remove strands from cardboard and tie separate 12-inch strand tightly around center of all strands, leaving ends for sewing. Fold all strands in half and tie another 12-inch strand around all folded strands ½ inch from first tie. Trim ends even.

FINISHING
Using 12-inch copper lengths from end of Tassel, tie 1 Tassel to center at each end of Scarf. After securing, run remaining loose ends down through center of Tassel to hide.

Weave in ends on Scarf, running ends through center of Tassel if necessary. ■

azure scallops

design by
REBECCA VELASQUEZ

SKILL LEVEL
◧■☐◻
EASY

FINISHED SIZE
Approximately 7 x 64 inches

MATERIALS
- J&P Coats Royale Fashion Crochet size 3 crochet cotton (150 yds per ball):
  3 balls #65 warm teal
- Size E/4/3.5mm crochet hook or size needed to obtain gauge

GAUGE
1 shell = 1 inch; 3 rows = 2 inches

PATTERN NOTE
Scarf is worked in 2 pieces. Each piece begins at the center and is worked outward.

SPECIAL STITCHES
Picot: Ch 3, sl st in 3rd ch from hook.

Shell: (3 dc, ch 2, 3 dc) in indicated st.

SCARF
FIRST HALF
Row 1: Ch 33, **shell** *(see Special Stitches)* in 8th ch from hook, *ch 1, **picot** *(see Special Stitches)*, ch 1, sk next 6 chs, shell in next ch, rep from * 3 times, ch 1, dc in last ch, turn.

Row 2: Ch 4, *shell in ch-2 sp of next shell, ch 1, picot, ch 1, sk next ch-1 sp, picot and ch-1 sp, rep from * across, ending last rep at **, dc in 3rd ch of beg ch-4, turn.

Rows 3–40: Rep row 2, **do not join or turn** at end of last row.

EDGING
Row 1: Ch 7, sk next ch-1 sp and next 3 dc, sc in next ch-2 sp, *ch 4, picot, ch 4, sk next 3 dc, next ch-1 sp, next picot, next ch-1 sp and next 3 dc, sc in next ch-2 sp, rep from * 3 times, ch 4, sk next 3 dc and ch-1 sp, dc in 3rd ch of beg ch-3, turn.

Row 2: Ch 1, sc in first dc, ch 4, sk next ch-4 sp, sc in next sc, *ch 4, picot, ch 4, sk next ch-4 sp, picot and ch-4 sp, sc in next sc, rep from * 3 times, ch 4, sk next ch-4 sp, sc in 5th ch of beg ch-7, turn.

Row 3: Ch 1, sc in first sc, ch 5, sk next ch-4 sp, sc in next sc, *ch 5, picot, ch 5, sk next ch-4 sp, picot and ch-4 sp, sc in next sc, rep from * 3 times, ch 5, sk next ch-4 sp, sc in next sc, turn.

Row 4: Ch 1, sc in first sc, ch 5, sk next ch-5 sp, sc in next sc, *ch 5, picot, ch 5, sk next ch-5 sp, picot and ch-5 sp, sc in next sc, rep from * 3 times, ch 5, sk next ch-5 sp, sc in next sc, turn.

Row 5: Ch 1, sc in next sc, ch 6, sk next ch-5 sp, sc in next sc, *ch 6, picot, ch 6, sk next ch-5 sp, picot and ch-5 sp, sc in next sc, rep from * 3 times, ch 6, sk next ch-5 sp, sc in next sc, turn.

Row 6: Ch 1, sc in next sc, ch 6, sk next ch-6 sp, sc in next sc, *ch 6, picot, ch 6, sk next ch-6 sp, picot and ch-6 sp, sc in next sc, rep from * 3 times, ch 6, sk next ch-6 sp, sc in next sc, turn.

Row 7: Ch 1, sc in next sc, ch 7, sk next ch-6 sp, sc in next sc, *ch 7, picot, ch 7, sk next ch-6 sp, picot and ch-6 sp, sc in next sc, rep from * 3 times, ch 7, sk next ch-6 sp, sc in next sc, turn.

Row 8: Ch 1, sc in next sc, ch 7, sk next ch-7 sp, sc in next sc, *ch 7, picot, ch 7, sk next ch-7 sp, picot and ch-7 sp, sc in next sc, rep from * 3 times, ch 7, sk next ch-7 sp, sc in next sc, turn.

Row 9: Ch 1, sc in next sc, ch 8, sk next ch-7 sp, sc in next sc, *ch 8, picot, ch 8, sk next ch-7 sp, picot and ch-7 sp, sc in next sc, rep from * 3 times, ch 8, sk next ch-7 sp, sc in next sc, turn.

Row 10: Ch 1, sc in next sc, ch 8, sk next ch-8 sp, sc in next sc, *ch 8, picot, ch 8, sk next ch-8 sp, picot and ch-8 sp, sc in next sc, rep from * 3 times, ch 8, sk next ch-8 sp, sc in next sc. Fasten off.

2ND HALF
Row 1: Join in opposite side of foundation ch, ch 4, shell in same ch as shell of First Half row 1, *ch 1, picot, ch 1, sk next 6 chs, shell in next ch, rep from * 3 times, ch 1, dc in last ch, turn.

Rows 2–40: Rep rows 2–40 of First Half, **do not join or turn** at end of last row.

EDGING
Rows 1–10: Rep rows 1–10 of First Half Edging.

Weave in all ends.

FINISHING
Optional: For a cleaner/crisper look, wet-block scarf. ■

cape cod circles

continued from page 9

Rnd 2: Ch 3, dc in same st as beg ch-3, 2 dc in each st around, join in top of beg ch-3. Fasten off. *(96 dc)*

CIRCLES 2–24
Rnd 1: Ch 24, being careful not to twist ch, **working through center of previous Circle** *(see Pattern Notes)*, join in first ch, ch 3, dc in same ch as beg ch-3, 2 dc in each ch around, join in top of beg ch-3. *(48 dc)*

Rnd 2: Ch 3, dc in same st as beg ch-3, 2 dc in each st around, join in top of beg ch-3. Fasten off. *(96 dc)*

Weave in ends after all Circles are finished and linked. ∎

picots in the sun

continued from page 15

TASSELS
Cut 31 12-inch strands. Fold 30 strands in half around 3 sk chs in row 1. Wrap rem strand around strands ¾ inch from fold. Rep Tassel in each rem group of 3 sk chs in row 1 and around each group of 3 sk chs in last row. Trim ends even. ∎

flouncy shades of blue

continued from page 26

Rnd 4: Sl st in next sp between tr, ch 4, tr in same sp as beg ch-4, working in natural sps between sts, 2 tr in each sp between sts around, join in top of beg ch-4.

Rnd 5: Sl st in next sp between tr, working in natural sps between sts, sl st in each sp between sts, around, join in beg sl st. ∎

mardi gras ribbon

continued from page 27

ASSEMBLY
Row 8 (joining row): Wrap Tube around all Strands, with rows 1 and 7 of Tube held tog, working through both thicknesses, sl st in each st across. Fasten off.

FINISHING
Optional: Gather both ends of 5 Strands tog (10 Strands), tie tog. ∎

STITCH GUIDE

STITCH ABBREVIATIONS

beg .... begin/begins/beginning
bpdc .... back post double crochet
bpsc .... back post single crochet
bptr .... back post treble crochet
CC .... contrasting color
ch(s) .... chain(s)
ch- .... refers to chain or space
previously made (i.e., ch-1 space)
ch sp(s) .... chain space(s)
cl(s) .... cluster(s)
cm .... centimeter(s)
dc .... double crochet (singular/plural)
dc dec .... double crochet 2 or more
stitches together, as indicated
dec .... decrease/decreases/decreasing
dtr .... double treble crochet
ext .... extended
fpdc .... front post double crochet
fpsc .... front post single crochet
fptr .... front post treble crochet
g .... gram(s)
hdc .... half double crochet
hdc dec .... half double crochet 2 or more
stitches together, as indicated
inc .... increase/increases/increasing
lp(s) .... loop(s)
MC .... main color
mm .... millimeter(s)
oz .... ounce(s)
pc .... popcorn(s)
rem .... remain/remains/remaining
rep(s) .... repeat(s)
rnd(s) .... round(s)
RS .... right side
sc .... single crochet (singular/plural)
sc dec .... single crochet 2 or more
stitches together, as indicated
sk .... skip/skipped/skipping
sl st(s) .... slip stitch(es)
sp(s) .... space(s)/spaced
st(s) .... stitch(es)
tog .... together
tr .... treble crochet
trtr .... triple treble
WS .... wrong side
yd(s) .... yard(s)
yo .... yarn over

YARN CONVERSION

OUNCES TO GRAMS	GRAMS TO OUNCES
1 .... 28.4	25 .... ⅞
2 .... 56.7	40 .... 1⅔
3 .... 85.0	50 .... 1¾
4 .... 113.4	100 .... 3½

UNITED STATES		UNITED KINGDOM
sl st (slip stitch)	=	sc (single crochet)
sc (single crochet)	=	dc (double crochet)
hdc (half double crochet)	=	htr (half treble crochet)
dc (double crochet)	=	tr (treble crochet)
tr (treble crochet)	=	dtr (double treble crochet)
dtr (double treble crochet)	=	ttr (triple treble crochet)
skip	=	miss

Single crochet decrease (sc dec):
(Insert hook, yo, draw lp through) in each of the sts indicated, yo, draw through all lps on hook.

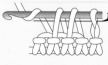

Example of 2-sc dec

Half double crochet decrease (hdc dec):
(Yo, insert hook, yo, draw lp through) in each of the sts indicated, yo, draw through all lps on hook.

Example of 2-hdc dec

Reverse Single Crochet (reverse sc):
Ch 1. Skip first st. [Working from left to right, insert hook in next st from front to back, draw up lp on hook, yo, and draw through both lps on hook.]

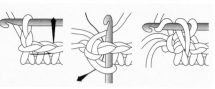

Chain (ch):
Yo, pull through lp on hook.

Single crochet (sc):
Insert hook in st, yo, pull through st, yo, pull through both lps on hook.

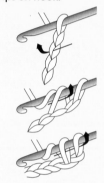

Double crochet (dc):
Yo, insert hook in st, yo, pull through st, [yo, pull through 2 lps] twice.

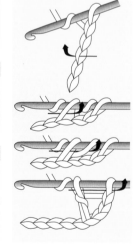

Double crochet decrease (dc dec):
(Yo, insert hook, yo, draw lp through, yo, draw through 2 lps on hook) in each of the sts indicated, yo, draw through all lps on hook.

Example of 2-dc dec

Front loop (front lp)
Back loop (back lp)

Front Loop   Back Loop

Front post stitch (fp):
Back post stitch (bp):
When working post st, insert hook from right to left around post st on previous row.

Back   Front

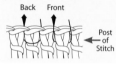

← Post of Stitch

Half double crochet (hdc):
Yo, insert hook in st, yo, pull through st, yo, pull through all 3 lps on hook.

Double treble crochet (dtr):
Yo 3 times, insert hook in st, yo, pull through st, [yo, pull through 2 lps] 4 times.

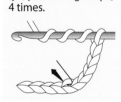

Treble crochet decrease (tr dec):
Holding back last lp of each st, tr in each of the sts indicated, yo, pull through all lps on hook.

Example of 2-tr dec

Slip stitch (sl st):
Insert hook in st, pull through both lps on hook.

Chain Color Change (ch color change)
Yo with new color, draw through last lp on hook.

Double Crochet Color Change (dc color change)
Drop first color, yo with new color, draw through last 2 lps of st.

Treble crochet (tr):
Yo twice, insert hook in st, yo, pull through st, [yo, pull through 2 lps] 3 times.

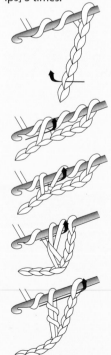

Metric Conversion Charts

METRIC CONVERSIONS

yards	x	.9144	=	metres (m)
yards	x	91.44	=	centimetres (cm)
inches	x	2.54	=	centimetres (cm)
inches	x	25.40	=	millimetres (mm)
inches	x	.0254	=	metres (m)

centimetres	x	.3937	=	inches
metres	x	1.0936	=	yards

INCHES INTO MILLIMETRES & CENTIMETRES (Rounded off slightly)

inches	mm	cm	inches	cm	inches	cm	inches	cm
1/8	3	0.3	5	12.5	21	53.5	38	96.5
1/4	6	0.6	5 1/2	14	22	56	39	99
3/8	10	1	6	15	23	58.5	40	101.5
1/2	13	1.3	7	18	24	61	41	104
5/8	15	1.5	8	20.5	25	63.5	42	106.5
3/4	20	2	9	23	26	66	43	109
7/8	22	2.2	10	25.5	27	68.5	44	112
1	25	2.5	11	28	28	71	45	114.5
1 1/4	32	3.2	12	30.5	29	73.5	46	117
1 1/2	38	3.8	13	33	30	76	47	119.5
1 3/4	45	4.5	14	35.5	31	79	48	122
2	50	5	15	38	32	81.5	49	124.5
2 1/2	65	6.5	16	40.5	33	84	50	127
3	75	7.5	17	43	34	86.5		
3 1/2	90	9	18	46	35	89		
4	100	10	19	48.5	36	91.5		
4 1/2	115	11.5	20	51	37	94		

KNITTING NEEDLES CONVERSION CHART

Canada/U.S.	0	1	2	3	4	5	6	7	8	9	10	10½	11	13	15
Metric (mm)	2	2¼	2¾	3¼	3½	3¾	4	4½	5	5½	6	6½	8	9	10

CROCHET HOOKS CONVERSION CHART

Canada/U.S.	1/B	2/C	3/D	4/E	5/F	6/G	8/H	9/I	10/J	10½/K	N
Metric (mm)	2.25	2.75	3.25	3.5	3.75	4.25	5	5.5	6	6.5	9.0

Scarves to Crochet is published by DRG, 306 East Parr Road, Berne, IN 46711. Printed in USA. Copyright © 2011 DRG.

RETAIL STORES: If you would like to carry this pattern book or any other DRG publications, visit DRGwholesale.com.

Every effort has been made to ensure that the instructions in this publication are complete and accurate.
We cannot, however, take responsibility for human error, typographical mistakes or variations in individual work.
Please visit AnniesCustomerCare.com to check for pattern updates.

ISBN: 978-1-59635-368-8   1 2 3 4 5 6 7 8 9